Handling An Explosive Kid

Ways To Handle An Explosive Kids. Ultimate Guide To Handle Explosive Kid

Donald E Simons

Table of contents

Chapter 1

What It Means To Have An Explosive Kid

How can I tell if my kid is explosive is a question that is often asked?

Of course, there is no blood test. The phrase "explosive" simply serves as a descriptor for children who express their dissatisfaction in considerably more severe ways than "regular" children does (shouting, yelling, spitting, punching, kicking, biting, slashing, and destroying property). To be quite honest, I've never found the word to be very funny.

First off, the word "explosive" indicates that these kids' outbursts are quick and unpredictably violent, yet most of the time that isn't the case.

Second, many behaviorally challenged children collapse as opposed to exploding when they get irritated (screaming, yelling, slapping, kicking, biting, spitting, and so on) (crying, sulking, pouting, having anxiety attacks, and being blue and withdrawn or cranky and irritable).

Therefore, despite the book's title, the techniques outlined here may be used with kids who are imploding, exploding, or doing a mix of the two.

These are kids that become very frustrated about little issues and react by weeping, yelling, shouting, kicking, punching, biting, spitting, damaging property, and worse. A kid whose frequent, violent outbursts make his or her parents angry, afraid, anxious, and helpless.

The majority of these parents have tried everything without success, including counseling, therapy, medicine, sticker charts, explanations, and punishment. They wonder why the methods that work for other children don't work for their child and are at a loss as to what to do in their place since they are unable to understand why their child behaves in the manner that he or she does.

There is too much conflicting information available for carers to know how to react, and the disagreements, backtalk, and (in some instances) physical aggressiveness make regular encounters into ongoing sources of irritation for both the kids and their caretakers.

These explosive children aren't attention-seeking, manipulative, or unmotivated, and their parents aren't passive, permissive pushovers, according to parenting expert and pioneer in the treatment of children with social, emotional, and behavioral challenges Donald E. Simons.

Instead, explosive children need a different parenting style since they lack several critical abilities in the areas of flexibility/adaptability, patience, and problem-solving.

Donald E. Simons, a parenting expert, is aware of how challenging parenting can sometimes be, particularly if or when your kid is throwing a temper tantrum. He compares a child's mounting rage to a shaken drink, he says:

"Consider rage like the bubbles in a two-liter bottle of soda. The volume of bubbles and internal pressure rise when the bottle is shaken.

You may release the pressure in the bottle without spilling any liquid if you gently unscrew the top (your self-control). Without removing the cap, the pressure within the bottle will continue to rise until it bursts, sending your cap flying off and making you lose control. A flying cap may cause damage and can even pose a threat. To put it another way, it's crucial to properly handle the child's negative emotions before they erupt.

Chapter 2

Symptoms Of Explosive Kid

The key indication of explosive disorder is a pattern of outbursts of fury that are out of proportion to the context or event that generated them. Explosive kids' parents should be aware that their kids' rage outbursts are unacceptable and they can't control their conduct throughout the episodes.

Explosive eruptions occur rapidly, with little or no warning, and generally last less than 30 minutes. These outbursts may occur often or be separated by weeks or months of nonaggression. Less severe verbal outbursts may occur in between instances of physical hostility. You may be impatient, impulsive, aggressive, or chronically furious most of the time. The angry bouts might be moderate or intense. They may entail harming someone seriously enough to need medical care or even cause death.

There is a range of symptoms that persons who have intermittent explosive disorder may present dependent upon individual genetic composition, development of social skills, coping techniques, the existence of co-occurring disorders, and use or addiction to drugs or alcohol. The following are some instances of numerous indications and symptoms that a person suffering from IED may exhibit:

- ❖ Temper outbursts.
- ❖ Verbal disputes may involve yelling and/or threatening people.
- ❖ Physically attacking people or animals, such as pushing, slapping, punching, or using a weapon to do injury.
- ❖ Property/object damage, such as throwing, kicking, or destroying things and slamming doors.
- ❖ Rage
- ❖ Irritability
- ❖ Increased energy
- ❖ Racing thoughts
- ❖ Tingling\sPalpitations
- ❖ Chest tightness
- ❖ Physical aggression
- ❖ Verbal aggressiveness
- ❖ Slapping, shoving, or pushing
- ❖ Physical fights

They may experience a feeling of relief and exhaustion following the event. Later, you may experience shame, regret, or humiliation.

Chapter 3

Understand Your Explosive Kid

Are you fatigued by the explosive actions of the children you love? First, I want to say I am proud of you. I know the weariness and stress that comes with raising a kid who feels out of control. The fact that you are reading this post shows you are searching for assistance and direction, and it means you are on your path to helping the children in your life. And trust me, you are probably already doing a better job than you think! Kids need you to show up more than anything! #truth.

As parents, grandparents, and carers we require skills. We need to keep trying something, anything, until we discover what soothes an explosive youngster. Do not give up. We are going to go into some strategies you may utilize the next time your youngster loses control of their emotions. It begins with emotional management for both the caregiver and the kid. When a parent is attuned to the kid and regulated inside their body, they may assist the youngster deal with stress via co-regulation.

Co-regulation is how youngsters learn in tandem with a secure and supportive adult to handle their strong emotions. If a youngster was affected by abuse and neglect, he or she may not have a functional model in their head for how to self-soothe and manage their emotions. This is where you come in.

As the adult you must establish a secure and caring environment for the kid balanced out with tough and good punishment. This may be extremely difficult to sustain if you are simultaneously suffering with your trauma, tiredness, or other mental health concerns. This is why it is so vital that caregivers and instructors take care of their mental well-being. Nobody can pour from an empty cup. Self-care is a buzz term during this epidemic, but what it truly means is that we must exercise the skills to manage our own emotions to raise or interact with children affected by trauma and loss successfully.

When a kid is in a state of wrath, it might help to recall that children never select a meltdown, the same way we wouldn't choose to throw a tantrum in front of our employer or parents. Explosive actions of a kid might activate the parents fear center in their brain and we frequently react with annoyance instead of reacting with care. Often when we are terrified, we display rage. When two individuals are in a condition of fear and fury, it is hard to learn and communicate. The urge for connection and trust dwells at the center of our existence. It is what we all need, even if we may be frightened.

Helping a kid with explosive behaviors doesn't require fear or shame-inducing punishments and discipline since it would simply provoke further outbursts. Explosive outbursts are a clue that the child's brain is "offline." In this condition, youngsters cannot hear you and make sense of the lesson you are attempting to teach about right and evil. This may seem ludicrous to you. You may feel youngsters need to learn their lesson in the moment or else they would become rebellious, difficult adults. I know this sensation all too well. It's the way we were taught in a society that employed incentives and penalties as tactics to acquire conformity among groups of youngsters.

With the latest information on how to help children manage after trauma, many caregivers feel trapped and don't know what to do. Most individuals previous to this age were raised with incentives and penalties, but now, this isn't working for the many youngsters afflicted by trauma and adverse childhood experiences (ACES). We have to do something different, and change is HARD. Our brain depends on prior experiences to conserve energy and make automatic judgments, particularly while under stress. The study suggests that punishments and incentives are unhelpful for around 50% of youngsters nowadays.

Chapter 4

Anger Management For Parents

Anger is a normal human emotion. Sometimes rage may be a good thing. For example, rage could give you the energy to get something done or to stand up for what you believe in.

Feeling angry and controlling your anger in constructive and healthy ways may also provide you the opportunity to set a good example for your children. For example, when you take a few deep breaths or walk away rather than explode, you show your children how to behave.

But rage may be bad, particularly if it occurs a lot or it gets out of control. Losing your temper when you're angry can make problems worse and lead to conflict with others. When you don't give yourself time to calm down, you might say or do unhelpful or hurtful things.

Also, children need to feel safe and secure to grow and develop, so being around a lot of conflict and yelling isn't good for them.

Raising children is a big and important job. It often involves balancing many different demands including work, family time, household chores, children's activities, and social activities. When you're in this situation, it's easy to lose patience and feel angry when things don't go to plan.

Sometimes you might feel angry or frustrated with your partner if you have one when you don't agree on decisions about raising children, discipline, and household chores. These sorts of disagreements can lead to conflict, especially if you're feeling undermined or unsupported.

Sometimes your child's anger or frustration can make you feel angry. For example, if your kid is upset and talks harshly to you or won't do as you ask, you could find yourself becoming angry too. You could find yourself attacking back at the moment and regretting it afterward.

And other circumstances might make you more prone to feel angry - including sickness, stress at work, financial troubles, lack of sleep, and not enough time for yourself.

It could assist you to know that many parents have weathered issues like these with the aid of family, friends, and health experts.

Consequences of extreme anger

Anger has different detrimental impacts on your health and those around you. Some of these repercussions are:

❖ ***Mental health:*** When you have anger stored up over a long length of time, it may evolve into major mental health disorders. These problems may include depression, drug addiction, and poor self-esteem.

❖ ***Relationships***: Losing your anger may destroy the connection between you and your children. In certain situations, when a youngster is exposed to furious outbursts, they may start to feel rejected and ostracized by their parent.

❖ *Physical Health:* Anger has detrimental impacts on the human body. Some health concerns such as heart failure, poor sleep, high blood pressure, and weaker immune systems have been associated with rage.

Recognizing indications of anger
Your body sends you early symptoms of rage. When you can spot these indicators, you can also take action to avoid your anger becoming out of hand.

Early indicators of rage include:

❖ Quicker heart rate or schurning stomach that is, feeling tight breathing flushing\stensing shoulders\sclenching jaw and hands\ssweating.
❖ Negative thoughts

❖ Negative thinking is quite prevalent when you're upset, and it might make your anger worse.

For instance, you can be stressed out after a challenging day at work. The moment you pick up your kids from school, an argument breaks out in the backseat, leaving you feeling irritated and agitated. You feel disappointed and upset when kids don't empty their lunchboxes and put their bags away when you arrive home.

Here are some unfavorable ideas you could have in this circumstance:

"No one ever assists me; I must do everything on my own."
You kids are so misbehaving,
I wouldn't be so furious if you acted better, you know.
Why do you want to make me angry?
In order to prevent losing your temper and erupting in fury, you need stop thinking ideas like this and take some action to calm yourself.

Ideas for managing anger quickly

First, recognize your rage.

Recognizing the early warning signs is the first step in controlling your anger. It's crucial to acknowledge your anger, even if it's only to yourself. For instance, "I can feel myself growing irritated here" or "This is making me upset."

Attempt to remain cool.

You may take a few steps to begin calming down as soon as you become aware of the beginning stages of rage.

Here are some techniques for calming down right now, particularly if you can't leave your child:

Try to breathe more slowly. Take a two-second breath in and a four-second breath out. Repeat this a few times to let your heart rate settle.
Try covering your ears or putting on noise-cancelling headphones for a while if your youngster is being really noisy. Then inhale slowly and deeply a few times.

Here are some suggestions to consider if you can get some time away from your child:

Engage in a calming activity, such as listening to music, reading a magazine, or just staring out the window.
Go for a run or a walk outside.
Shower with warm water.
Share your feelings with a buddy.
Before going away, make sure your youngster is in a secure location. It could be possible to ask someone to keep your youngster while you take a little break someplace peaceful.

Your heart rate lowering and your muscles relaxing are indications that you're calming down.

Consider the circumstance.

It could be beneficial to think back on what just occurred after you feel like your emotions have subsided. This may help you draw lessons from the scenario and deal with similar ones more effectively in the future. Think about it:

How crucial is this? Why did I become so angry over it?

How do I want to handle this circumstance?

Is there anything I should be doing about this, or can I simply let it go?

providing children with a positive model of anger management

It's OK to be upset, but it's not acceptable to injure or shout at someone.

If you apologize for being upset, it suggests that anger is inappropriate. Therefore, it is preferable to apologize for screaming or losing your anger. Your children will learn from this that although it's OK to feel angry sometimes, finding constructive methods to deal with anger is more important.

What to do if you can't control your rage

There will always be situations in which you struggle to control your rage and shout or say regrettable things.

When this occurs, it's a good idea to pause and consider what to say to your spouse or children. Here are a few concepts:

"I apologize for becoming angry. I'll go away the next time so I can relax early.
I'm sorry for shouting. Can we discuss what occurred just now?
'I apologize. Even though I was upset, I should have avoided saying it. I ought to have taken a break and collected myself before we discussed it. Children may suffer a great deal as a result of parental rage.

If a parent is furious, the kids could blame themselves. Additionally, a child's stress levels brought on by a parent's rage may have an impact on how their brain develops. Being around rage as a child increases the likelihood of developing mental illness later in life.

Parental rage may lead to verbal or emotional abuse of a kid. A youngster may believe it is their fault and feel unworthy if a parent speaks nasty words to them out of rage.

Children may behave badly, rudely, or violently in response to their parents' anger. Children might also become sick, isolate themselves from others, or have trouble sleeping.

Anger that escalates into physical violence might endanger a kid severely. Throwing, shaking, or beating a newborn may result in serious harm, incapacity, or even death.

Chapter 5

Secret To Successfull Parenting Of An Explosive Kids

Screaming fighting. Destructive behavior. Volatile moods. Do your child's fury and wrath make you feel fatigued and out of control?

Don't worry too much about a diagnosis. Getting a diagnosis "certifies" that there's something different about your kid, but it doesn't teach you exactly why your child is explosive.

Childhood psychiatric diagnoses are labels that are ascribed to groups of bad behavior. The behaviors themselves, however, are the manner in which your kid is letting you know that he or she is having problems fulfilling specific expectations.

If your kid is striking, spitting, biting, kicking, throwing objects, yelling, cursing, or damaging property, the actions all convey the same thing.

Explosive children lack critical cognitive abilities. Research done over the past 40 to 50 years shows us that behaviorally problematic youngsters lack critical abilities, including flexibility/adaptability, frustration tolerance, and problem-solving.

This is why they burst or display problematic behaviors when specific circumstances require certain talents. Expectations surpass skills. The collision between expectations and abilities happens commonly among behaviorally challenged youngsters, and their responses tend to be more intense.

But these kids aren't always challenging: their troubles are situational, restricted to specific settings and expectations.Figure out the abilities your kid lacks and which expectations he has problems satisfying.

Responding to your child's wrath with anger is not the solution. Instead, it's ideal to create what I call a fury plan so that you know precisely how you will properly address the next outburst or temper tantrum. A fury strategy puts you in charge of yourself and the circumstance.

The following stages are the cornerstone of this plan:

1. Ensure the Area Around Your Child Is Safe

Ensure that the space surrounding your kid is secure and that no one can be injured if and when your child lashes out. Remove yourself and any siblings from the area.

Reduce any stimulus in their surroundings. Turn off the TV, and dim the lights. The objective is to let your youngster tire themselves out. This phase applies to teenagers as well as to young children.

2. Focus on Being Calm

Even if emotions are running high, attempt to calm yourself down. Talk to your child in a calm tone, even if you feel like screaming at them.

Tell your child that his or her behavior is unacceptable and that you'll speak with them when they've calmed down.

Model good behavior for your child. Remember, kids, learn from their parents, which is another reason you want to remain calm. You're teaching them appropriate ways to manage stressful situations.

3. Don't Respond to Name-Calling or Verbal Abuse

If your child is screaming things at you, calling you names, or saying you're "the worst parent in the world," do not respond. And don't take it personally. Instead, leave the room or send them to their bedroom.

Also, don't shout back at your kid since it will draw you into their wrath and make you the main center of their anger.

4. Talk Later, When You're Both Calm

The moment to discuss this is when you and your kid are both calm. If they're shouting in their room, they should not be receiving your attention, period.

Don't worry if it looks as though you're ignoring the improper conduct.

What you are doing is not responding to the shouting. Or, to phrase it another way, you are not allowing your child's ranting to rule your behavior.

Later, when things are quiet, and at the moment of your choice, you may explain to your kid that their conduct was not appropriate. Tell them there are other ways to cope with rage than losing control. But do it on your terms, not your child's. After all, you're the CEO of your home.

You could also have your youngster make apologies if they damaged anything or injured someone else. If your kid is extremely young, you may ask them to create a picture that reads, "I'm sorry." If your kid is older, urge them to do something more significant for the person they've hurt.

5. Give Consequences for the Behavior, Not the Anger

Don't offer punishments because your youngster got furious. Instead, offer punishments for your child's particular improper conduct, such as verbal abuse, physical violence, or property damage.

Your youngster needs to realize that it's appropriate to be furious. We all feel furious from time to time. And occasionally we shout. Nevertheless, we need to learn to handle ourselves responsibly when we feel furious.

In other words, let your kid know that anger is natural and that there will always be things in life that make them furious. Then highlight that they're responsible for and will be held accountable for any improper conduct coming from their rage.

6. Be Consistent

If your youngster has just begun to lash out in wrath when irritated, this strategy going to work quite well—especially after you go through it a few times.

Your calm and matter-of-fact reaction is going to show them that explosive fury is not the way to cope with their displeasure. And it won't get them what they want.

But if the behavior has been going on for a long time and it's more entrenched, ready to go through your fury plan frequently until your kid learns to regulate his anger better.

Made in United States
North Haven, CT
03 January 2023

30479775R00017